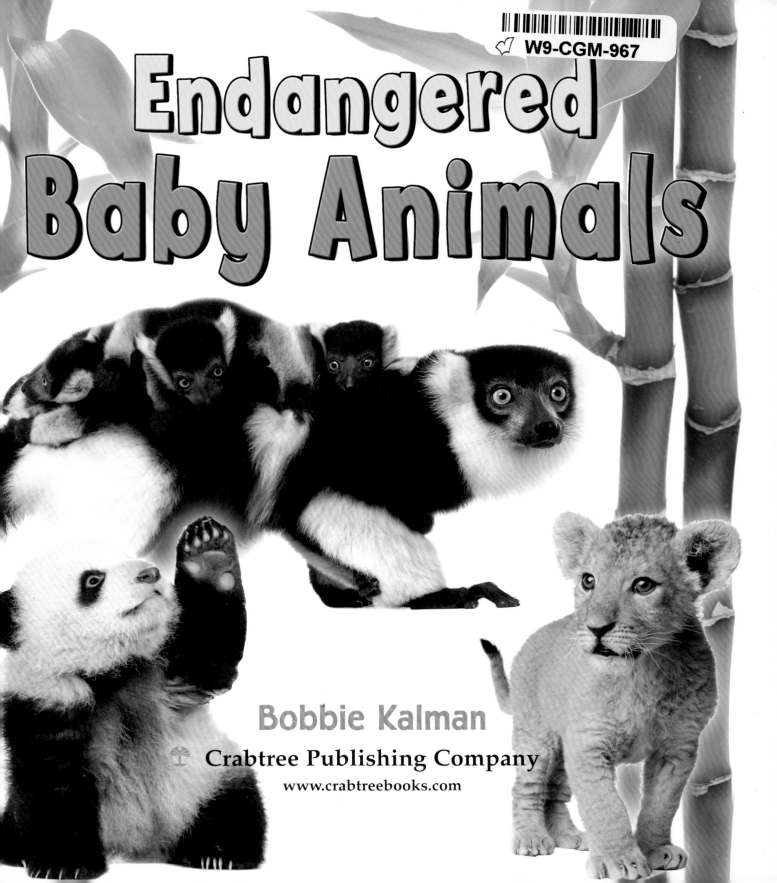

Endangered Baby Animals

Bobbie Kalman

Crabtree Publishing Company

www.crabtreebooks.com

It's fun to learn about **Baby Animals**

Created by Bobbie Kalman

Dedicated by Crystal Sikkens
For Nicholas Gerrit Haanstra,
may the world of books bring you wonder and delight

**Author and
Editor-in-Chief**
Bobbie Kalman

Editors
Kathy Middleton
Crystal Sikkens

Design
Bobbie Kalman
Katherine Berti
Samantha Crabtree
   (logo and front cover)

Photo research
Bobbie Kalman

Print and production coordinator
Katherine Berti

Prepress technician
Katherine Berti

Illustrations
Bonna Rouse: pages 20, 22, 23

Photographs
BigStockPhoto: pages 16, 24 (polar bears)
Hung Chung Chih/Shutterstock.com: page 11
All other images by Shutterstock

Library and Archives Canada Cataloguing in Publication

Kalman, Bobbie
   Endangered baby animals / Bobbie Kalman.

(It's fun to learn about baby animals)
Includes index.
Issued also in electronic formats.
ISBN 978-0-7787-4076-6 (bound).--ISBN 978-0-7787-4081-0 (pbk.)

   1. Endangered species--Juvenile literature. 2. Animals--Infancy--
Juvenile literature. I. Title. II. Series: It's fun to learn about baby
animals

QL83.K345 2012   j591.68   C2011-907669-1

Library of Congress Cataloging-in-Publication Data

Kalman, Bobbie.
  Endangered baby animals / Bobbie Kalman.
    p. cm. -- (It's fun to learn about baby animals)
  Includes index.
  ISBN 978-0-7787-4076-6 (reinforced library binding : alk. paper) --
ISBN 978-0-7787-4081-0 (pbk. : alk. paper) -- ISBN 978-1-4271-7888-6
(electronic pdf) -- ISBN 978-1-4271-8003-2 (electronic html)
  1. Endangered species--Juvenile literature. 2. Animals--Infancy--Juvenile
literature. I. Title.

QL83.K365 2012
578.68--dc23

2011046088

Crabtree Publishing Company

www.crabtreebooks.com   1-800-387-7650

Printed in Canada/012012/MA20111130

Published in Canada
Crabtree Publishing
616 Welland Ave.
St. Catharines, Ontario
L2M 5V6

Published in the United States
Crabtree Publishing
PMB 59051
350 Fifth Avenue, 59th Floor
New York, New York 10118

Published in the United Kingdom
Crabtree Publishing
Maritime House
Basin Road North, Hove
BN41 1WR

Published in Australia
Crabtree Publishing
3 Charles Street
Coburg North
VIC 3058

What is in this book?

Endangered animals

Thousands of **species**, or kinds, of animals are in danger of becoming **extinct**. When an animal has become extinct, no one has seen it anywhere for more than 50 years, and we will never see that animal again.

In the wild

Many animals that can be seen in zoos or protected parks called **preserves** are at risk of dying out in the **wild**. The wild is a natural place that people do not control. The chart on the right explains the words scientists use to describe animals that are in danger of becoming extinct.

Words to know

Scientists use these words to describe animals that are in danger in the wild.

vulnerable Describes animals that may become endangered because they are facing certain risks

endangered Describes animals that are in danger of dying out in the wild

critically endangered Describes animals that are at high risk of dying out in the wild

extinct in the wild Describes animals whose only known living members are in captivity, such as at a zoo

Baby animals in danger

Baby animals face the same dangers as adult animals do—and many more. They are small and cannot take care of themselves the way adult animals can. Find out why the baby animals on this page, and others, are endangered and how you can help them.

This Sumatran tiger cub is critically endangered.

This lion cub is vulnerable.

This giant panda cub is endangered.

This African elephant calf is vulnerable.

This baby Sumatran orangutan is critically endangered.

This Amur leopard cub is critically endangered.

This African penguin chick is endangered.

What is a mammal?

Many endangered animals are **mammals**. Mammals have hair or fur on their bodies. They are **warm-blooded**. The bodies of warm-blooded animals always stay about the same temperature, whether they are in the hot sun or in cold water. Mammal babies are **born**, or come out of their mothers' bodies live.

*Mammal mothers feed their babies milk from their bodies. Drinking mother's milk is called **nursing**. This elephant calf is nursing. Elephant calves nurse for two or more years.*

Endangered elephants

Elephants are the biggest mammals on land. They are vulnerable. Most elephants are losing their **habitats**, or natural homes. People are building farms and cities on the land where these big animals once lived. **Poachers** kill elephants to get their ivory tusks. Poachers are people who hunt animals illegally so they can sell their body parts. Many baby elephants lose their mothers when the mothers are killed by poachers.

ivory tusk

A calf is carried inside its mother's body for almost two years before it is born. When mother elephants die, their babies often die, too. This calf's mother was killed. The baby is being cared for by humans because it cannot care for itself.

Poaching is against the law, but many people still want to buy things made from ivory, like this tusk with carvings on it. As long as people buy ivory, poachers will keep killing elephants.

Endangered primates

Most orangutans are critically endangered. They are losing their forest homes.

Primates are the smartest mammals. We are primates, too. Primates have arms, legs, hands, and feet, with fingers and toes for holding objects. Monkeys and apes are two kinds of primates. Monkeys have tails, but apes have no tails. Most primates live in forests in warm places. Apes live mainly in Africa and Asia. Chimpanzees, orangutans, and gorillas are all endangered apes.

baby orangutan

Chimpanzees are endangered, and most gorillas are critically endangered. Baby apes are trapped and sold as pets. Adult apes are often hunted for their meat and other body parts.

baby gorilla

young chimpanzee

Two groups of monkeys

There are two groups of monkeys: Old World monkeys and New World monkeys. Old World monkeys live in Africa, Asia, and Europe. New World Monkeys live in Central and South America.

Douc langurs are Old World monkeys. They are endangered because many forests are being cut down in Asia, where they live.

Golden lion tamarins are New World monkeys that live in the forests of South America. Not long ago, they were critically endangered, but people are helping them, and more babies are now being born.

Lemur babies

Lemurs are primates called **prosimians**. Most of the world's lemurs live in Madagascar, an island that is part of Africa. Lemurs live high up in trees and eat mainly fruit. The mother and baby lemurs on this page are called black-and-white ruffed lemurs. They are critically endangered. They are losing their forest homes and are eaten by many **predators**, such as hawks and civets. Predators are animals that hunt and eat other animals. A civet looks like a cat with a pointed nose.

Protection for pandas

The giant panda is a well-known endangered animal. Its picture is used as a symbol to remind people to help all endangered animals. Panda mothers have very few cubs, so their **population**, or number, does not grow.

Panda cubs are able to climb trees, even as babies. They need to eat a lot of bamboo.

Bamboo eaters

Pandas eat a lot of bamboo, but bamboo forests are being cut down. Most pandas live on preserves, or parks where they are protected from poachers. Poachers kill pandas for their fur.

This panda cub lives on a preserve.

Tigers and leopards

Wild cats are cats that do not live with people. Many tigers, leopards, and other wild cats have lost their habitats. People often hunt these cats because the cats eat farm animals when they cannot find other animals to eat. People also hunt the cats for their fur and other body parts. Two critically endangered wild cats are the Sumatran tiger and Amur leopard.

This Sumatran tiger cub, and the one above, live in Asia on the island of Sumatra in the country of Indonesia. The forest homes of these tigers have been cut down to plant palm trees, from which palm oil is made. There may be fewer than 400 of these tigers left.

Most endangered cats

Amur leopards are among the most endangered wild cats in the world! There are fewer than 35 of these cats left in the wild. The baby leopards you see on this page live in zoos. The cubs in the wild live in the forests of eastern Russia. Amur leopards have become extinct in China and South Korea. Some live in special parks that protect them from poachers that hunt them for their fur, bones, whiskers, and meat.

Threatened lion cubs

(above) This lion cub is hiding in the grasses of its habitat.
(left) This cub is just six weeks old.
(below) How many of these cubs will become adults?

Wild lions live in Africa and in Asia. African lions are vulnerable. Many live in **savannas**, or large, hot, grasslands. Lion cubs face several dangers in their savanna home. Many are eaten by jackals, leopards, eagles, and snakes.

The last to eat

The youngest cubs often starve to death because they are the last ones to eat, after the bigger cubs have eaten. Only one-fifth of the lion cubs born live past the age of two years!

Vulnerable cheetah cubs

Cheetahs are the fastest land animals on Earth. They can run 70 mph (113 km/h). Like lions, cheetahs live in African savannas and are also vulnerable. Cheetah cubs must learn a lot in their first months of life, such as how to hunt and how to avoid predators.

*Cheetah cubs are born with a **mantle** of soft fur on their necks and along their backs.*

Cheetah mothers live alone with their cubs. When they leave the cubs to go hunting, the cubs are often eaten by predators.

This cheetah cub is learning how to hunt.

Cheetah cubs hide in the grasses to stay safe.

Polar bear problems

Polar bears are mammals that live in the Arctic, an area in the northern part of Earth. The Arctic is made up of the Arctic Ocean and the lands around it. Some of these lands include northern Canada and Alaska. Most polar bears live on **pack ice**, or thick pieces of ice that float in the ocean. In summer, the bears move onto land to find food. Their land habitat is called the **tundra**.

There are no trees on the tundra because it is very cold and windy there.

Melting ice

Polar bears are vulnerable because Earth is becoming warmer. In the Arctic, warmer temperatures mean that the pack ice is thinner and is melting earlier than usual.

Hunting and eating

Polar bears hunt seals that live under the ice. When the seals come up for air at their breathing holes, polar bears grab them. Hunting this way takes less energy than chasing the seals in the ocean. Polar bears also use the ice as "tables" on which they eat the seals they have caught. Less ice means less food for polar bear mothers and their cubs.

When polar bears cannot find food in the ocean, they look for it on land in garbage dumps like this one.

Because so much sea ice is melting, pieces of ice float farther apart. Polar bears must swim farther to hunt food. Many cubs drown because they cannot swim far enough to reach a piece of ice.

17

More endangered babies

The endangered baby animals in this book are mainly mammals. Many other kinds of animals are also endangered, such as fish, birds, and **reptiles**. Birds have feathers, and reptiles have skin made of **scales**, or bony plates.

The sun parakeet lives in South America. It is endangered because it is trapped and sold as a pet. Many kinds of parrots are sold as pets.

African gray parrot chicks are found in the rain forests of West and Central Africa. More than one-fifth of these birds are taken from their homes to become pets because they can say hundreds of words and understand their meanings.

Hermann's tortoises live in southern Europe. Their greatest threat is from destruction of their habitats. They are also trapped and sold as pets.

African penguin chicks are endangered for several reasons. The baby birds are killed by predators such as seals, sharks, and orcas. Many penguins also die because of pollution, such as oil that is dumped out of ships.

Alligator snapping turtles grow to be huge turtles that live in rivers and lakes in the southern United States. They are vulnerable because they are hunted for their shells and meat. They are often caught on fishing lines, as well.

This crocodile **hatchling**, or baby, is a Cuban crocodile. Cuban crocodiles are reptiles. They live only in two small wild areas in Cuba. They are critically endangered due to hunting and because they live in such small natural habitats.

Sea turtles in danger

Sea turtles live in oceans. This baby hawksbill sea turtle is critically endangered.

Sea turtles are reptiles. Most reptiles **hatch**, or break out of eggs. There are eight species of sea turtles. All are endangered, but the hawksbill, Kemp's ridley, and leatherback are critically endangered. Sea turtles are hunted for their meat and beautiful shells.

Baby sea turtles hatch from eggs on beaches. When they hatch, they have to walk to their ocean homes. Birds swoop down and eat them on their way to the water. Only one out of 1000 make it. This baby sea turtle is a leatherback. It is almost home!

The Kemp's ridley is the smallest sea turtle.

Helping animals

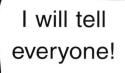

You can help endangered animals. Learn as much as you can about them and tell others.

- Make posters of endangered animals and put them on your school walls.
- Do not buy endangered animals as pets. The more endangered pets people buy, the more will be trapped.
- Start a school newspaper to teach other students about endangered animals.

Where on Earth?

This map shows where some of the endangered animals in this book live.

1. polar bear (Arctic)
2. alligator snapping turtle (southern United States)
3. Kemp's ridley sea turtle (Atlantic Ocean and Gulf of Mexico)
4. Cuban crocodile (Cuba)
5. leatherback sea turtle (Atlantic, Pacific, and Indian oceans)
6. hawksbill sea turtle (warm parts of Atlantic, Pacific, and Indian oceans)
7. golden lion tamarin (Brazil in South America)
8. Hermann's tortoise (southern Europe)
9. chimpanzee (west Africa)
10. gorilla (central Africa)
11. lion (central and southern Africa)

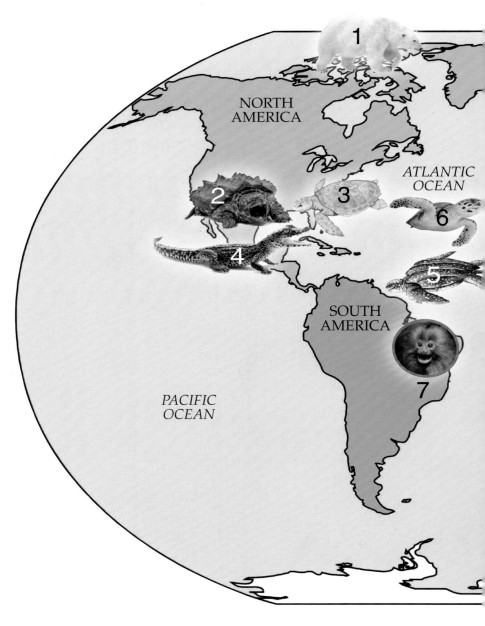

12. cheetah (most of Africa)

13. elephant (Africa and Asia)

14. African penguin (south-western Africa)

15. black-and-white ruffed lemur (island of Madagascar in Africa)

16. giant panda (central and western China)

17. orangutan (island of Sumatra in Indonesia)

18. Sumatran tiger (Sumatra, Indonesia)

19. Amur leopard (eastern Russia)

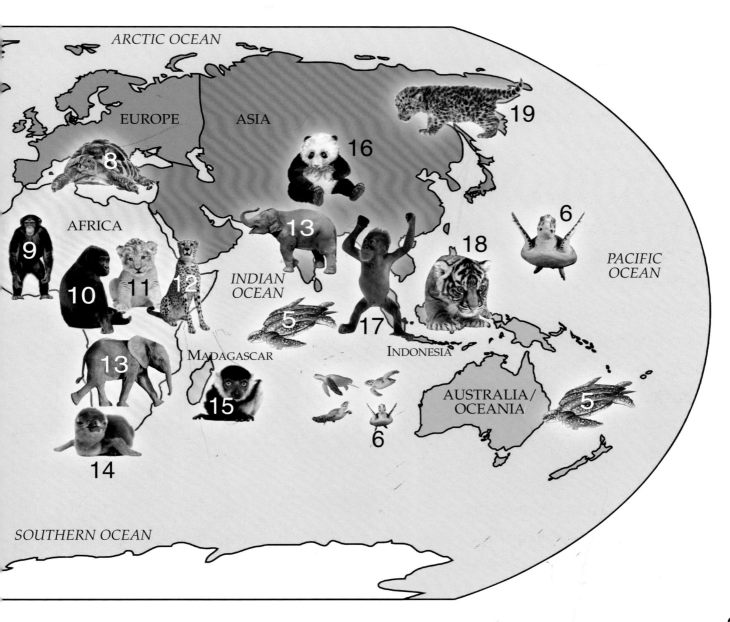

Words to Know and Index

birds
pages 5,
18, 19, 23

cheetahs
pages 15, 23

elephants
pages 5, 6, 7, 23

leopards
pages 5, 12, 13, 14, 23

lions
pages 5,
14, 15, 22

pandas
pages 5,
11, 23

polar bears
pages
16–17, 22

primates
pages 5, 8–9,
10, 22, 23

reptiles
pages 18,
19, 20, 22

tigers
pages 5,
12, 23